The Monster Flute Method Book

A Beginner's Guide

By Anna Meyer

Illustrations by Laura Dalgarno-Platt

©2019 aemeyer

Table of Contents

Preface	2
Meet the Monsters	3
Getting Started with Music Theory	4
Music Notes are Named for Fractions	6
Time Signatures	7
Ok, Let's Play	9
Putting the Flute Together	9
Holding the Flute	10
Making a Sound on the Flute	11
Equivalents in Music – Notes and Rests	18
Sharps, Flats, and Naturals	22
Keys and Key Signatures	24
Study in the Key of F	25
Study in the Key of G	26
Tonguing and Articulation	27
Dotted Notes	29
Dots (and Ties)	30
Familiar Tunes and Folk Songs	31
Dynamics	34
Slurs	35
Triplets	37
Arpeggios	39
Compound Meter	40
Cut Time	43
Single Eighth Notes and Rests	44
Sixteenth Notes and Beyond!	46
Syncopation and Dotted Eighths	48
Expanding our Technique Through Time, Key, and Range	50
Flutists' Favorites	53

Appendix

Vocabulary	58
Chart of Musical Terms	60
Order of Sharps and Flats	61
Circle of Fifths Chart	62
Major Scales	64
Fingering Chart	66
Flashcards	69

    Cut out these pages and use these flash cards to help you practice note reading.

Preface

Dear Teachers –

This book was designed with the beginning flute student in mind. After over twenty years of teaching and pulling my favorite things from different books, I decided it was time for me to write a book that was a compilation of my teaching style, philosophy, and personality.

I love the method of some of the tried-and-true books but found that my youngest students lose interest very quickly. Some of the more engaging books tended to be geared toward the beginning ensemble experience and start off in B♭. I wanted something that would start the students off with a little bit of theory, so their understanding of musical terms was in a place to set them up for success once they pick up the flute. Feel free to jump in and out of the first several pages of theory as you feel you need to in your lessons. Inundating a student with too much theory and not enough playing will lose their interest. I played around with integrating theory with more playing at the beginning, but all the basic concepts go so well together, that I decided to keep them all in one spot and allow you to use your best judgement in utilizing this information. Additionally, I wanted to start my students off in C major, helping them to learn more concretely and practically why we have sharps and flats. Finally, I wanted a book that would entertain the students and give them something to look forward to when they open it.

I hope you will find Mavis, Joel, and Sam to be good companions as you guide your students along this learning path. Their personalities have developed over the course of getting this book into print in a way that makes me excited to hand them off to you, and I hope you enjoy their antics.

Thank you to all of my teachers, who instilled such high-quality teaching techniques in me, and especially to David Cramer for his guidance and suggestions on this book. Special thanks to Laura for her brilliant illustrations in making Mavis, Joel, and Sam come to life, and to my husband Erik, for his patience in teaching me all about music notation software.

Through this journey, I hope you turn into a monster of a flute player, but more importantly, that you find joy and delight in learning this instrument.
    ~Anna.

Meet the Monsters

"Hi, I'm Mavis"

I am a little shy, and sometimes new things make me a little hesitant, but I am very willing to learn.

"Hi! I'm Joel"

I am adventurous! I love to jump in feet first. I'm very excitable, because I just want to learn it all right now! (Also, Mavis and Sam will tell you that I'm a little bit of a know it all.)

"Hello, I am Sam"

I am the one that keeps Joel on the right track. They call me the informant. I like to keep my information concise. Just the facts.

Getting Started
Use this section of the book to get familiar with some of the musical terms we use all the time. Knowing these symbols and terms will help you when you pick up the flute.

The Monster Code - What the symbols mean

 **Treble or G Clef** - The flute plays in Treble Clef. The clef is what tells us which notes are on which lines and spaces. Other clefs look like

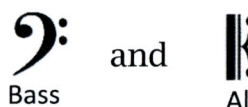

 **Time Signature** - tells us how the measures are organized and how many beats to count. The time signature breaks the music down into smaller pieces called **measures** so they are easier for us to understand. It also affects the feel of a piece. For example a waltz is in 3, whereas a march is in 2 or 4. Here's how we write it:

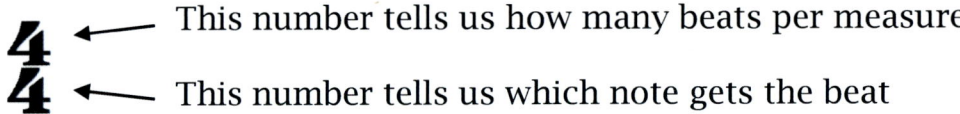
This number tells us how many beats per measure

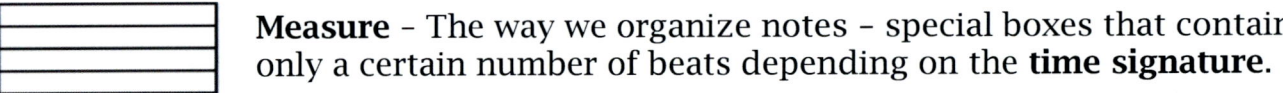
This number tells us which note gets the beat

Measure - The way we organize notes - special boxes that contain only a certain number of beats depending on the **time signature**.

Learning to play an instrument can feel like you are getting a lot of information all at once, and that is certainly a little bit true only because most of these terms are ones you have likely never heard before. Everything is new. However, Mavis, Joel, and Sam are here to help you get the most out of learning to play the flute and to help you feel excited and interested as you learn. If you forget what one of the terms in bold type means, use the vocabulary list in the back of the book to help you. Remember that this is a new language you are learning and that it is a skill that takes time. So take a deep breath and know that you too can be a monster flute player!

Music Notes are Named for Fractions

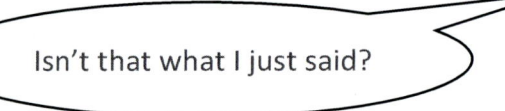 

○ This is a **whole note** because it takes up the WHOLE measure. It gets 4 beats.

♩ This is a **half note**, because it takes up ½ of the measure. It gets 2 beats.

♩ This is a **quarter note** because it takes up ¼ of the measure. It gets 1 beat. There can be 4 of these in each measure.

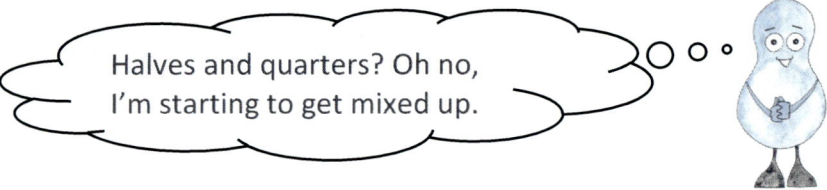

Look how it works. We can use any combination of these notes, as long as they equal 4 when added together!

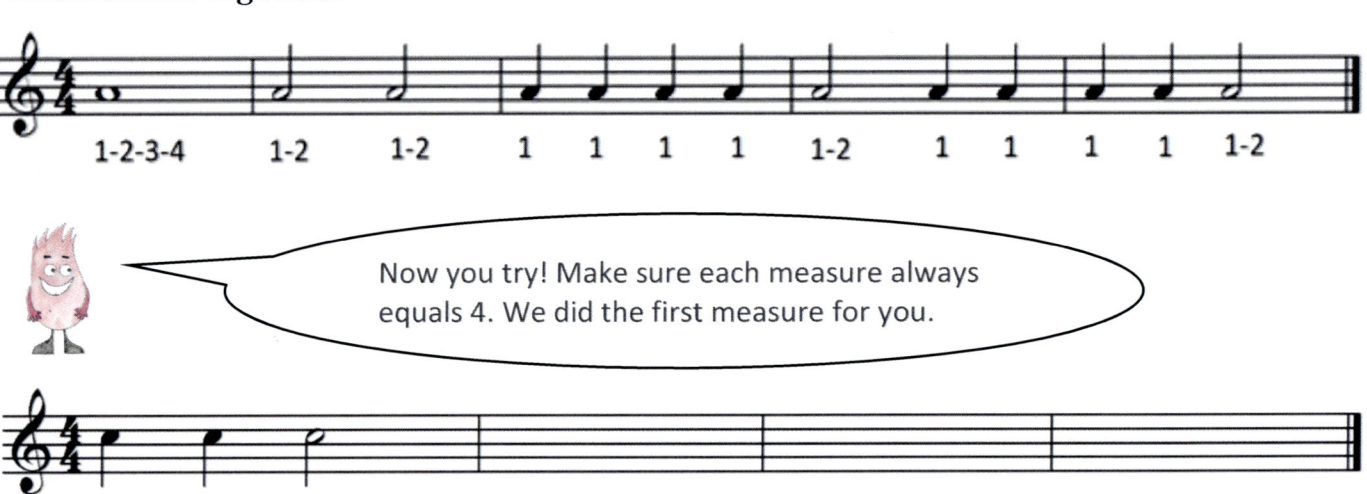

Now you try! Make sure each measure always equals 4. We did the first measure for you.

Time Signatures

We talked a little about what a time signature is on p. 4. Now let's talk about what the numbers mean.

Here come the fractions, oh no!

4 The number of beats in each measure
4 The type of note that gets the beat

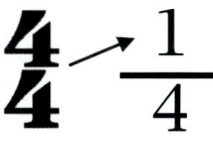 (¼) quarter note gets the beat. We count this ♩ or something that equals it (like 𝅗𝅥+♩+♩) until we get to 4, then we start a new measure.

You already knew that, but now, we can change the numbers on the top to make a different time signature.

3 ← How many beats per measure?
4 ← Quarter note still gets the beat.

Three!

Example:

We can't use a whole note in this time signature, because a whole note = 4, and that's too many beats.

This top number really can be anything, but you will most frequently see these

4/4 3/4 2/4   and occasionally   **5/4 6/4**

4/4 ← Is sometimes called **common time** and looks like this → **C**

This is a *lot* of information to take in at once. Hang in there. We're getting to the good stuff.

Try writing a few measures of your own and watch out for the top number!

Try your own time signature. Keep the bottom number a 4, but you can choose any number for the top! Don't forget to write it in, and remember, you can use any combination of notes as long as the total number of beats is the same as that top number.

Now, can you put in the counts under your composition? Follow the example of the counts on the previous page. See if you can put in the counts for the measures you wrote at the top of the page too.

Ok, Let's Play!

Putting the flute together
The flute has three parts:

Just like me!

Nope, we are just a head and some feet.

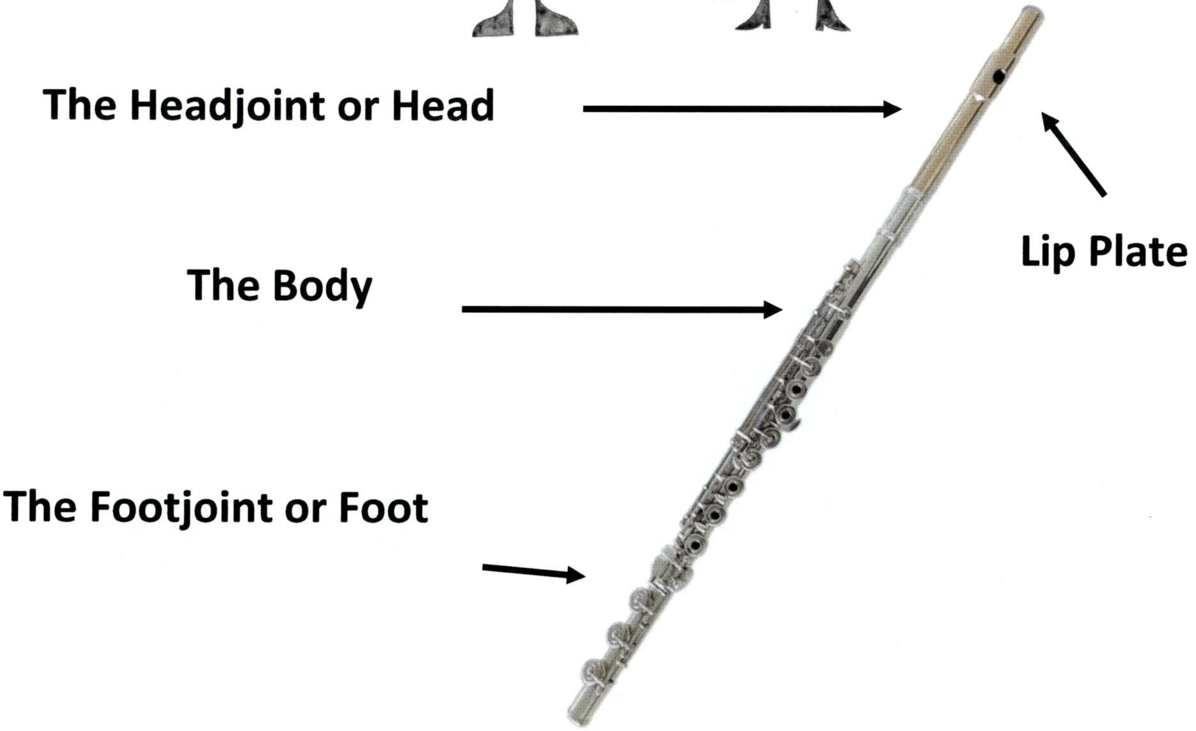

The Headjoint or Head

Lip Plate

The Body

The Footjoint or Foot

Head to Body - Line up the hole in the lip plate with the middle of the *third* key. Make sure the headjoint is not pushed all the way in. It should be out about ½ an inch.

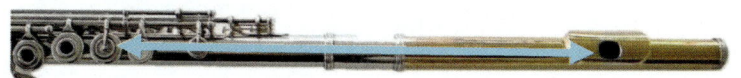

Body to Foot - The rod of the body lines up in the *middle* of this key on the footjoint.

Do you have a really long pinkie on your right hand?

Or a really short one?

You can move the footjoint a little bit either way to make it more comfortable. Just be sure you can still reach the rollers. You'll need those later!

Holding the Flute

Left Hand   ### Right Hand   ### Lips

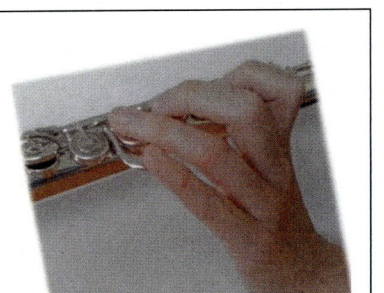 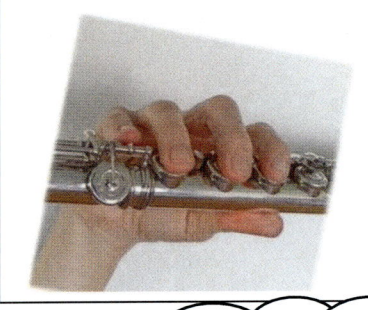 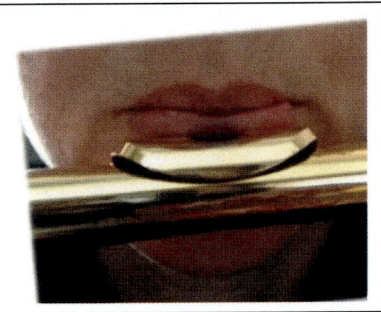

Right hand looks a lot like a puppet. Nice and relaxed.

Just like blowing through a straw – no tension in your cheeks!

Be sure to skip a key between the first and second fingers!

Keep the flute nice and low on your bottom lip.

Make sure you have a nice cradle in the crook of your left pointer finger for the flute to sit in.

Making a sound on the Flute

Flute is one of the hardest instruments to start, so if you can't get a sound at first, don't worry! Just keep experimenting with finding the perfect place on your face for the shape of your lips and chin. We all have differently shaped faces, so your **embouchure** may not look exactly like the one in this picture.

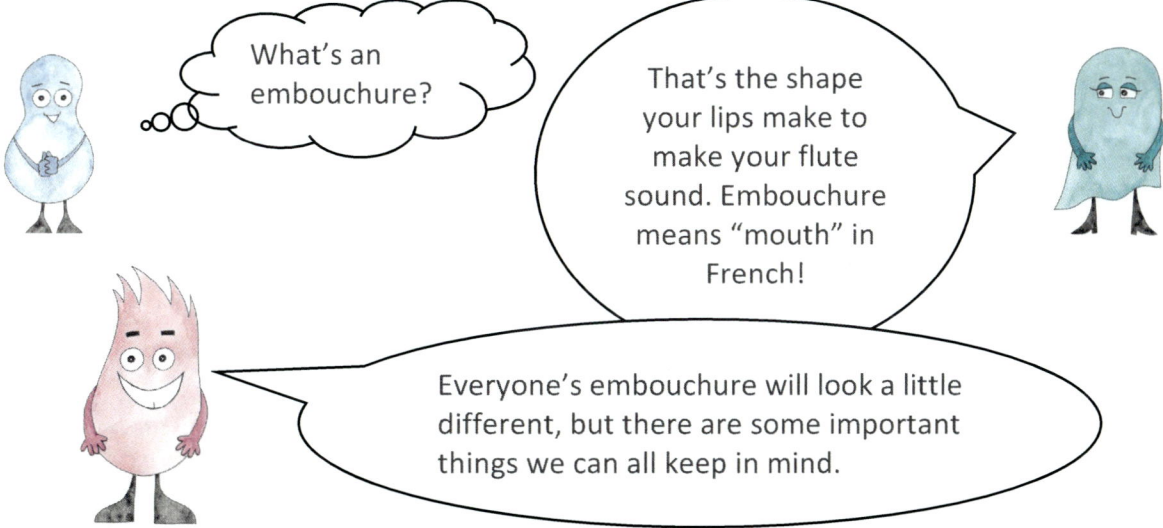

Joel's tips for making a flute sound

1. Using the index finger of either hand, find the indentation just below your bottom lip on your chin. Feel that? That's where the flute goes. Place the lip plate right here. If you have fuller lips, you may need to put the flute a little bit higher (actually on your bottom lip) but most of us will have it just below the lip.

2. Form the word "pooh" with your lips, as pictured previously, and press the air out of your lungs into the flute. Try to think of really pressing the air out, don't just breathe out. We really have to have strong air moving through the flute!

3. Playing the flute takes a LOT of air. Keep this in mind. Keep the air moving over that little hole in the headjoint. As you progress, you will learn that sometimes we put more air into the flute and sometimes we put more air across the hole, but there is always air going in AND going across!

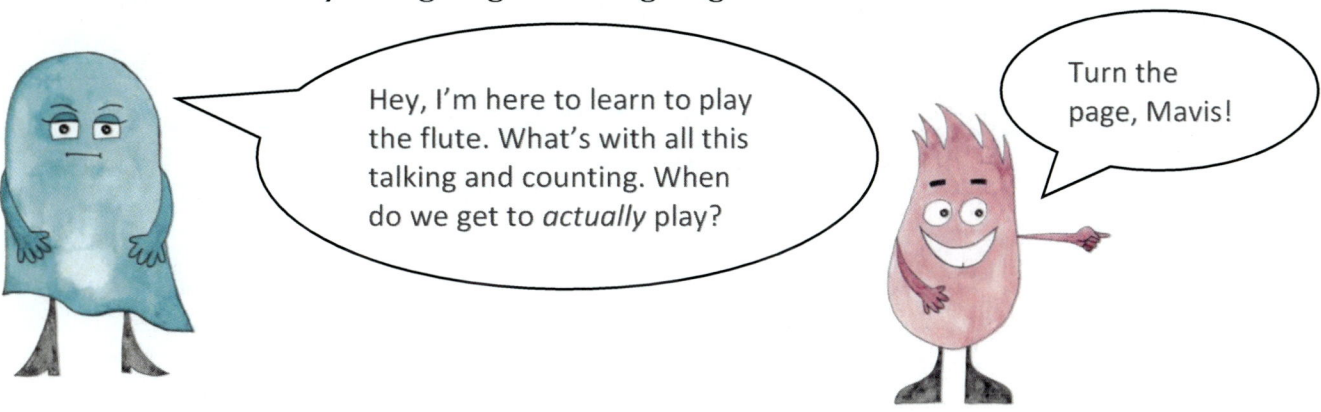

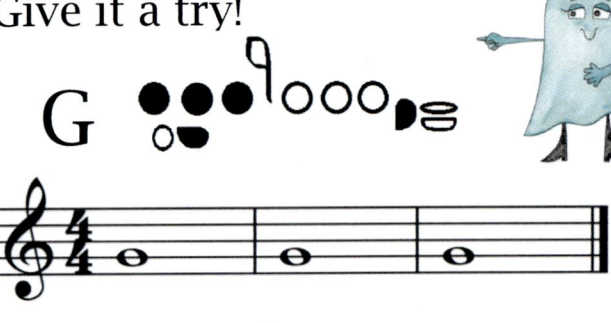

Give it a try!

G

F

Try them together.

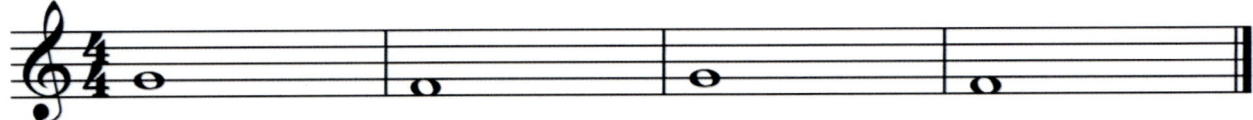

Now the other way.

You can remember the notes on the spaces with this sentence:
   Flutes **A**re **C**ertainly **E**xciting

You can remember the notes on the lines with this sentence:
   Elephants **G**ot **B**ig **D**irty **F**eet

The **Musical Alphabet** only has **seven** letters **A to G**, then we repeat A to G again. Count forward to go up (A-B-C-D-E-F-G), and count backward to go down (G-F-E-D-C-B-A)

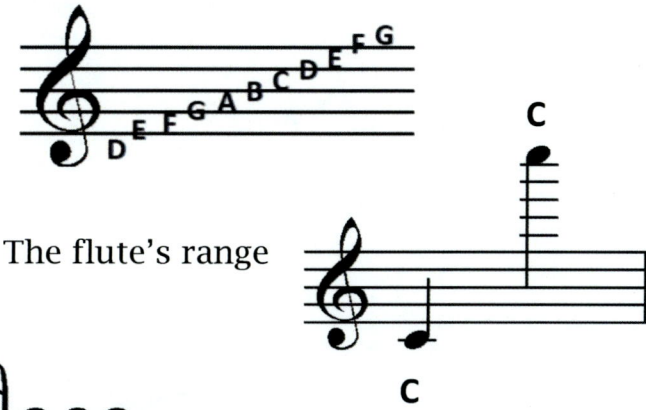

The flute's range

Let's keep going!

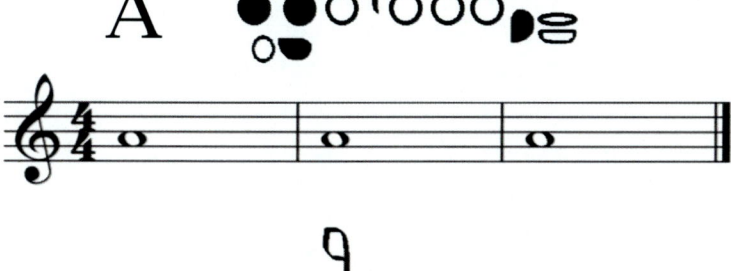

 Here are some exercises to help you practice G, F, A and B. See if you can guess the name of the tune for #3. Let your eyes and your ears work together.

1.

2.

Can you name this tune?* _____

3.

4.

Joel's Rhythm Challenge – Can you clap these rhythms while counting aloud? Try playing them after you've done that and see how fast you can go!

5.

New Note E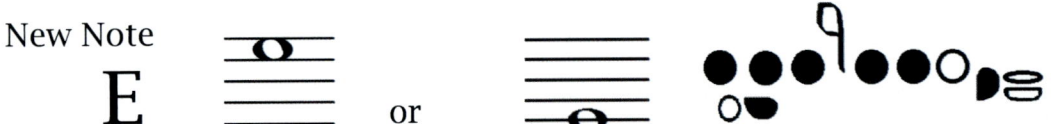

6.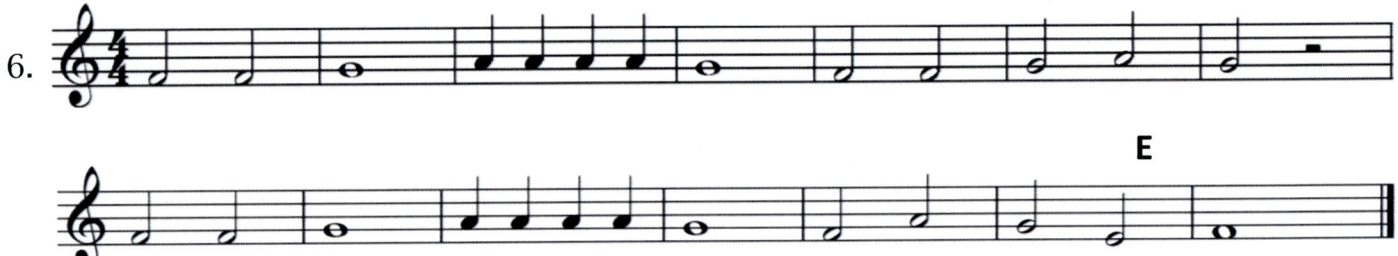

*answer to #3 Name that Tune
Hot Cross Buns

1.

2.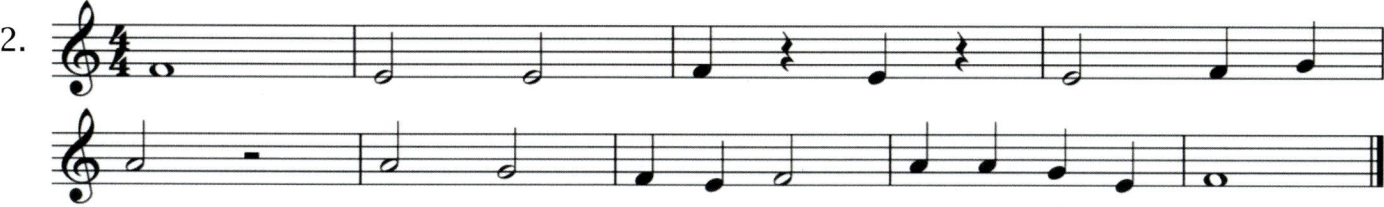

Rhythm Study – Write in the counts, clap, then play

3.

Count   1   2   3   4

4.

Count   1   2   3   4

5.

Count   1   2   3   4

Equivalents in Music

Check out this chart to see how music notes add up to form other notes. For example – a whole note is made up of two half notes, four quarter notes, or eight eighth notes.

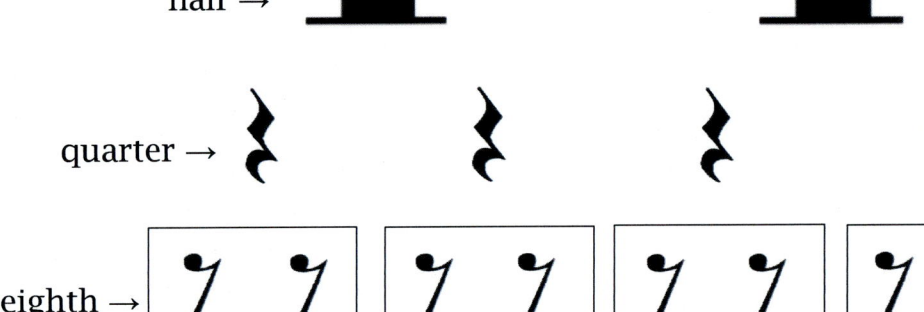

* For those of you who are super savvy at math, here's an interesting fact for you: Each note or rest on these rhythm charts is exactly half the value of the note or rest above it. Whole=4; Half=2; Quarter=1; Eighth=1/2. See the example below.

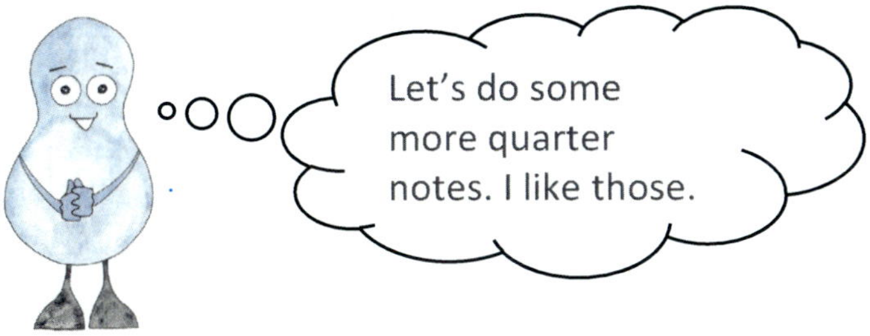

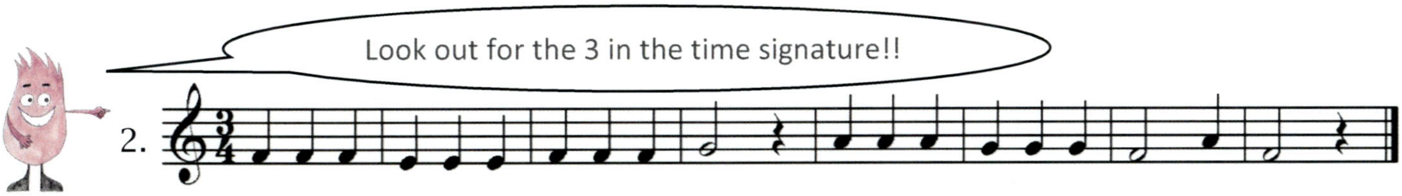

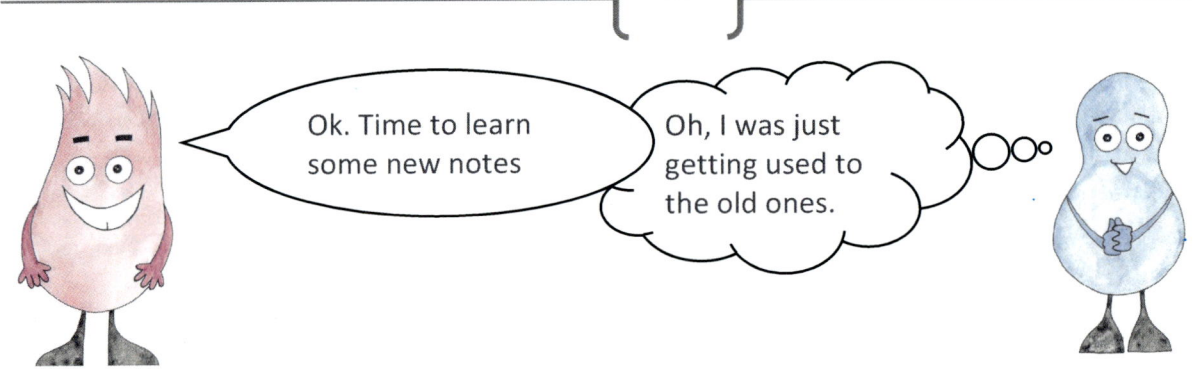
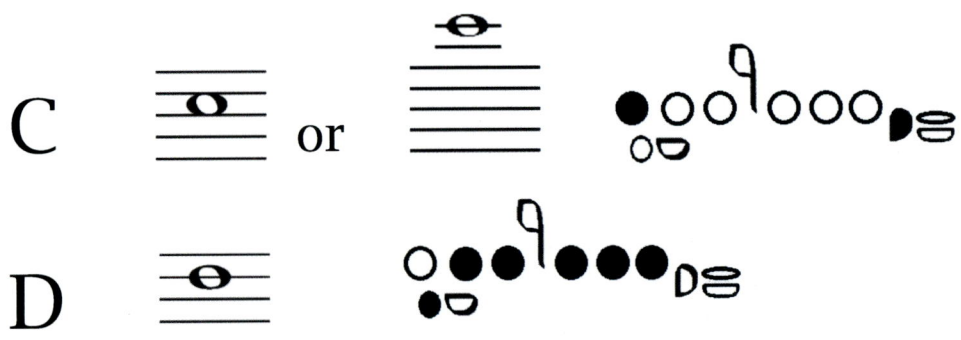

Let's start with D

1.
2.

Now for C

3.
4.

And put them together!

5.
6.

Challenge: Mirror Image

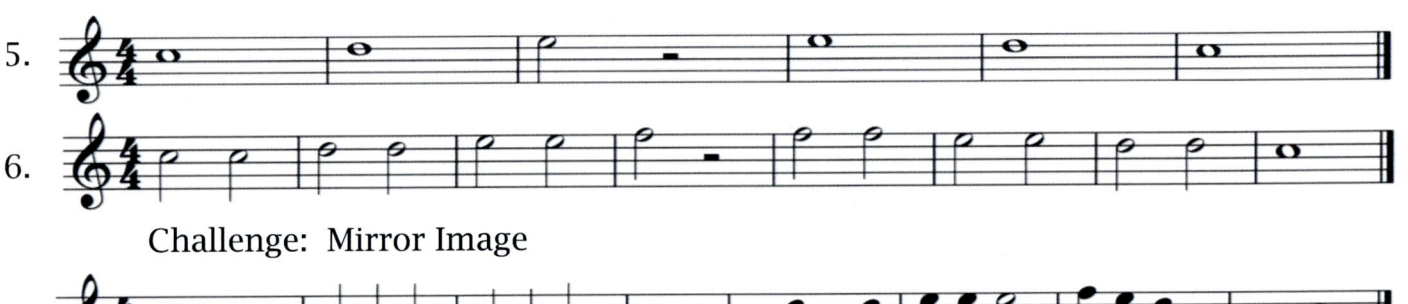

Sharps, Flats, and Naturals

If you think about how a keyboard has white and black keys, a flat (♭) or sharp (#) is a flutist's way of playing the black keys. Up until now, we have been playing all **"naturals"** (♮) or the white keys.

A **flat (♭)** takes a note and lowers it by one half step. A half step on the keyboard is the distance between two keys (usually white to black or black to white, but sometimes white to white!). Find B on the keyboard. Now find A. Do you see the black key in between B and A? This is called B♭ (or A# - all black keys have two names. Any time a note has two names, this is called **enharmonics**). We can actually add a flat to *any* note to make it go down a ½ step. Or we can add a **sharp (#)**.

It's a hashtag!

Mavis is right. It's the same symbol we use for a hashtag, but in music we call it a sharp and it *raises* a note by a ½ step. See if you can find F, now see if you can find F#, one black key to the right. This symbol (♮) makes a sharped or flatted note go back to **natural** (or white keys).

Same tune, different sound
Let's use what we learned about sharps and flats while we look at this famous tune.

Goodnight, Jack.

Bb   or

F#   or

Lights out, Jack.

Go to sleep, Jack!   G   A

Jack's Bad Dream

Wait...that's not right.

It's ok, Sam. We call it **minor**. Lots of music is written in minor, but this one is supposed to be **major**, that's why it sounds funny.

Keys and Key Signatures

A **key** is a specific collection of notes. Right now we are working mostly in major keys. Let's look at F Major. Here are the notes that make up the key of F Major. When we put them in order, we call them a **scale**.

In this case we start on F, go up to F, and come back down. There is one flat - B♭. We can do the same thing starting on any note. If we start and end on C, there are no sharps or flats, starting and ending on G there is one sharp. There are twelve major scales, each one starting on a different note. You can find them all in the back of this book. There's also a **circle of fifths** chart, which helps you figure out how many sharps and flats each scale has.

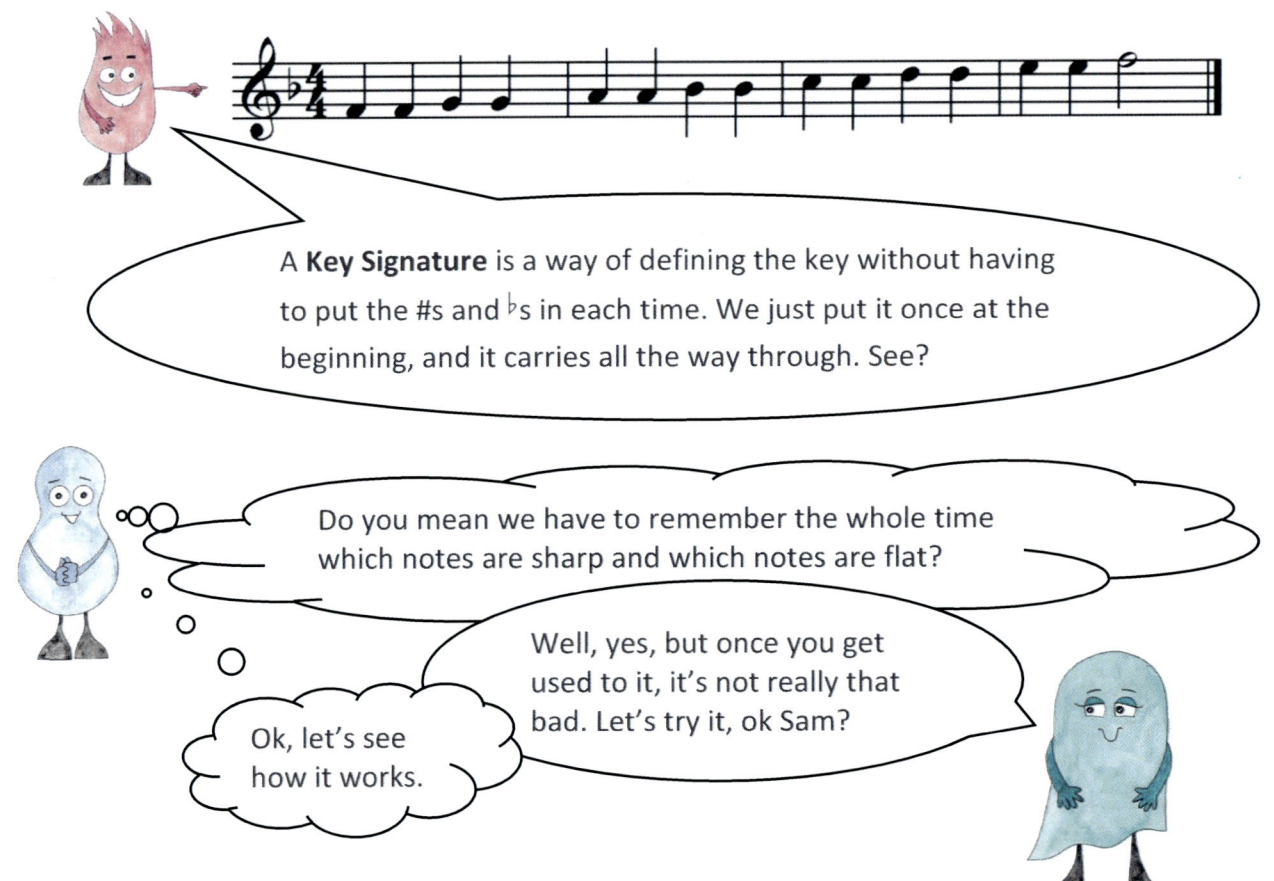

A **Key Signature** is a way of defining the key without having to put the #s and ♭s in each time. We just put it once at the beginning, and it carries all the way through. See?

Do you mean we have to remember the whole time which notes are sharp and which notes are flat?

Well, yes, but once you get used to it, it's not really that bad. Let's try it, ok Sam?

Ok, let's see how it works.

Tonguing and Articulation

It takes a little getting used to, but we can do it! Here's how. Put your tongue on the back of your teeth right where your teeth meet your gums. There's a little fleshy bump there. This is the spot your tongue will tap to start the sound. Try saying, "Too, too, too." That's all it is. Now say "too" with just the "t" sound, don't actually phonate. Put your hand in front of your lips and feel how the tongue cuts the air. Now you've got it! Shall we try it with the flute?

This is a technique we will continue to use for the rest of the time we are playing the flute. It's OK if you forget. It will eventually feel more natural and a little more normal.

One of the great things about playing music is playing with friends. Find a friend or your teacher and see how you do with these. Or, record yourself playing one part and play a duet with yourself. Watch out for the key signature, and don't forget to use your tongue!

See Saw

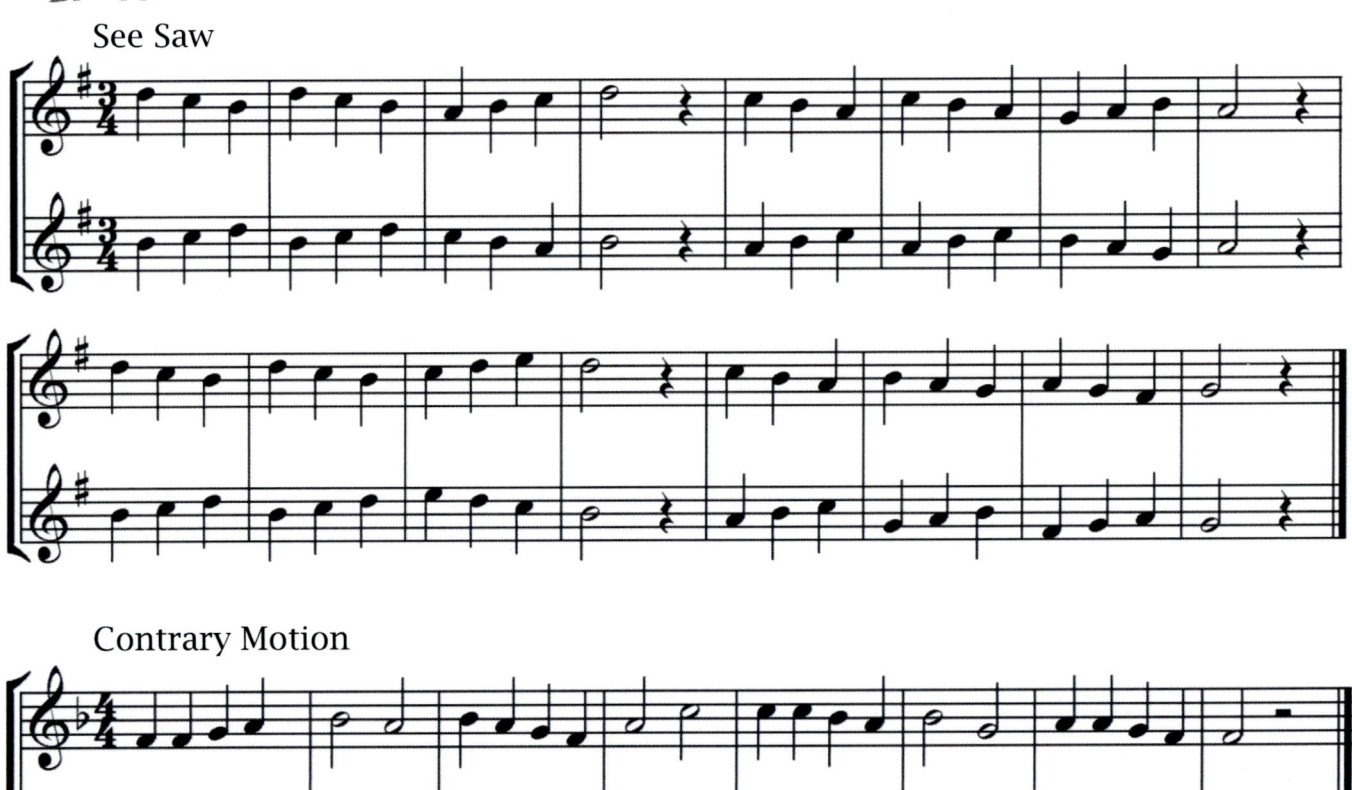

Contrary Motion

Do you recognize this one? It's from Handel's oratorio *Judas Maccabeus*.

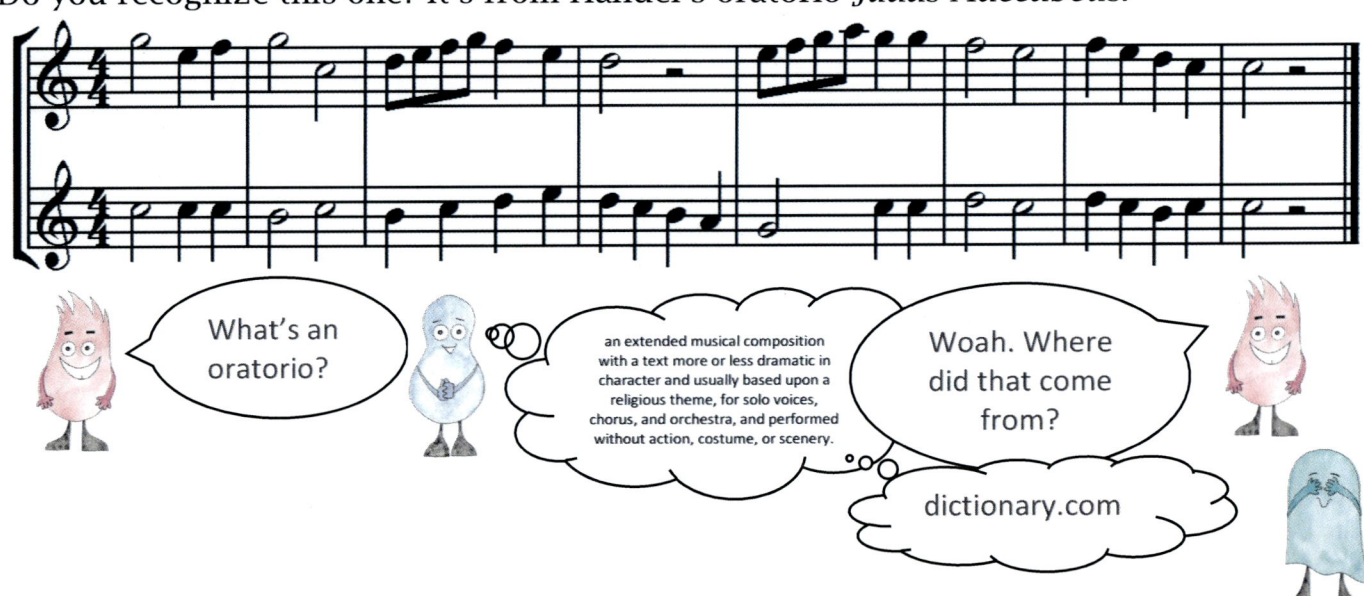

What's an oratorio?

an extended musical composition with a text more or less dramatic in character and usually based upon a religious theme, for solo voices, chorus, and orchestra, and performed without action, costume, or scenery.

Woah. Where did that come from?

dictionary.com

Dotted Notes

We are going to learn about dots, and this is easiest to explain with donuts. Here is a half note: 𝅗𝅥 It gets two beats. Now I add a dot to that note. It looks like this 𝅗𝅥. and it gets **three** beats. So the dot adds half of the value of the original note back to that note.

Ok, so 𝅗𝅥 = 2 = 🍩 🍩   and the • = ½ of 2, which is 1 = 𝅘𝅥 = 🍩, so…
🍩🍩 + 🍩 = 🍩🍩🍩   or 𝅗𝅥 + 𝅘𝅥 = 𝅗𝅥.   or 2+1=3

Here's where it gets tricky: when we have to start cutting donuts in half. Remember that the dot (•) adds *half the value of the original note back to that note*. Let's try it with a quarter note.

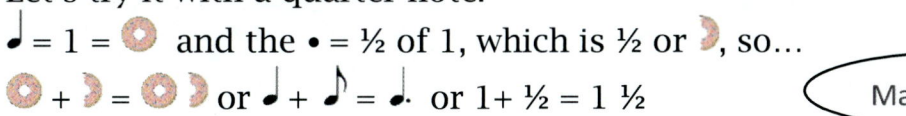

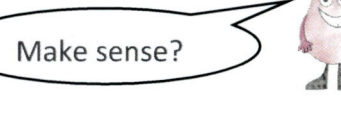

Yes! Let's try it. Let's start with the dotted half, it's easier.

More fractions? Will this never end!?

Dots (and ties)

 Oh no! We forgot to tell you about **ties**! A tie ⌢ is a symbol we use in music to join or add the value of multiple notes with the same pitch together. A dot can be a short hand way of writing a tie. They look different, but they end up sounding the same when you play them.

Try this scale using ties first, then using dots.

1. 1-2 (3) 4   1-2 (3) 4   1-2 3 4   1-2-3 4   1-2-3 4   1-2-3 4   1-2 3 4   1-2-3 4

2. 1-2-3 4   1-2-3 4   1-2 3 4   1-2-3 4   1-2-3 4 1-2-3 4   1-2 3 4   1-2-3 4

Here are two more for you to try – Can you write the counts in under these?

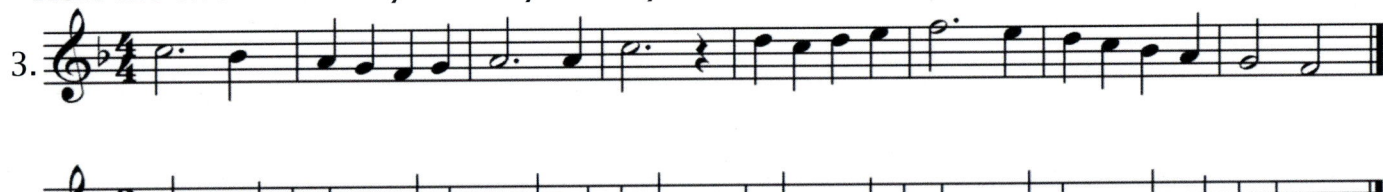

Try it with tied quarter notes.

count: 1   (2) + 3 (4) +   1   (2) + 3   4   1   (2) + 3 (4) +   1   (2) + 3   4

And now dotted quarter notes.

Familiar Tunes and Folk Songs

Use these folk tunes to help you practice some of the new notes and rhythms we have been talking about. Watch out for the key signatures, and don't forget to be using your tongue to start the notes.

Yankee Doodle

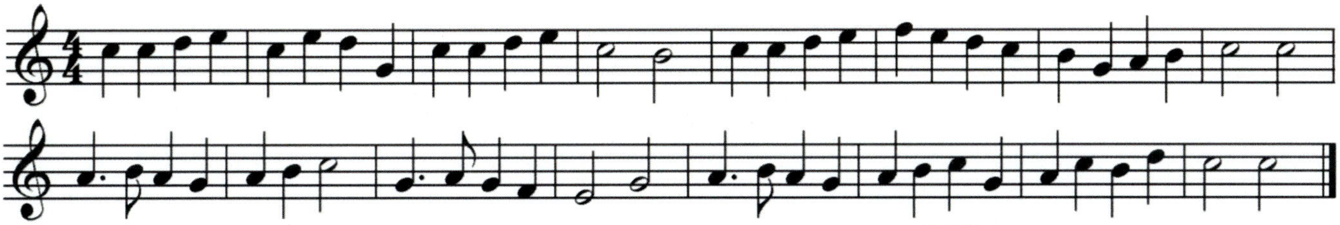

Time for some new notes!

Eb

C#

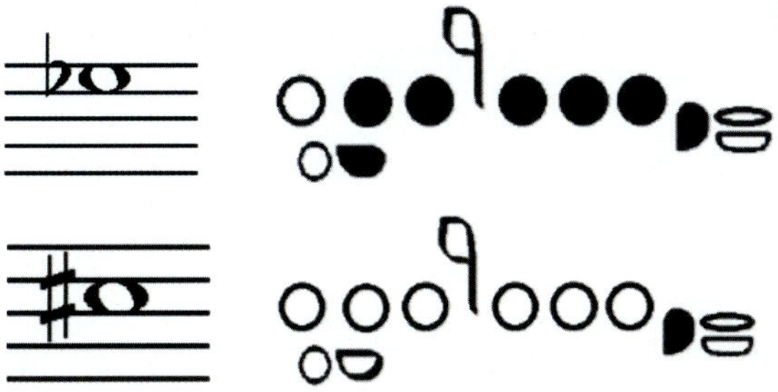

Woah, woah! How are you even supposed to hold that?!?

That little cradle in your left index finger needs to really be doing its job!

I've Been Working on the Railroad

 Hey, what's this: ♮ ? It's a **natural**. It cancels out a sharp or a flat, in this case, the C#.

Simple Gifts

Dutch Folk Song

When the Saints Go Marching In (African American Spiritual)

Morning Mood by Edvard Grieg (Norway)

Chiapanecas, a Mexican Folk Tune - *Play this for a friend or a teacher and see if you can get them to clap only on the rests. Switch parts and see if YOU can do it.*

Ezekiel Saw the Wheel – African American Spiritual

Theme from Antonin Dvorak's *New World Symphony*

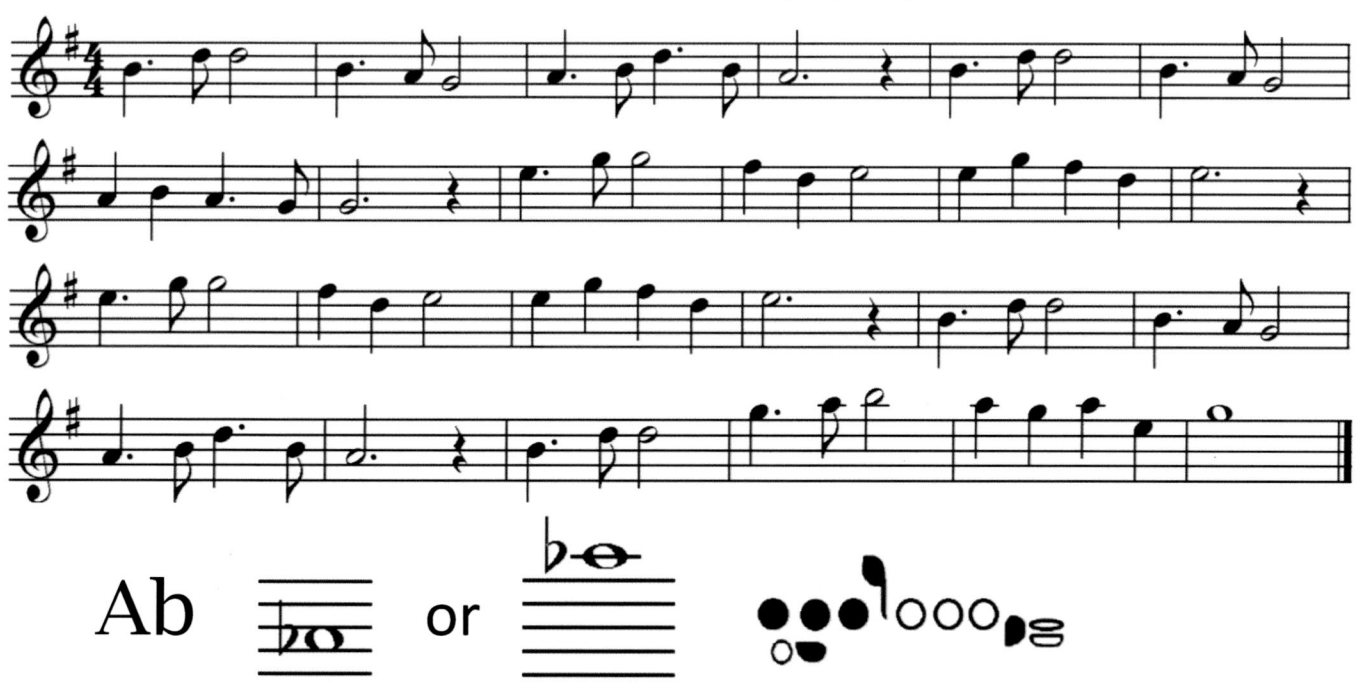

Ab

Theme from Jean Sibelius' *Finlandia*

Dynamics

"Do you want to learn about dynamics?"

"I'm sorry, I could barely hear you. What did you say?"

I said, "Do you want to learn about **dynamics**?"

Wow. *That* was loud.

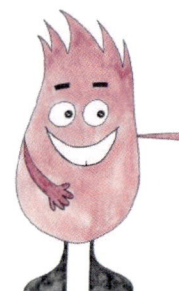

That's exactly what dynamics are! They tell us how loud or soft to play. Look at Mavis. She's got it.

mp   mf
p   f
pp   ff

Oh look, here they all are in a chart. And you know what? I don't see *any* fractions!

Symbol	Italian name	English meaning
pp	*pianissimo*	very soft
p	*piano*	soft
mp	*mezzo piano*	medium soft
mf	*mezzo forte*	medium loud
f	*forte*	loud
ff	*fortissimo*	very loud
cresc.	*crescendo*	get louder
decresc.	*decrescendo*	get softer

That's right, Sam, no fractions here! We also have symbols to tell us to get louder and softer, and they have Italian names too.

crescendo - get louder

decrescendo - get softer

Slurs

Do you remember when we talked about **ties** a little while back? Here we are going to learn about **slurs**, which look a lot like ties.

Yeah, they do. What's the difference, Mavis?

Well, a **tie** connects two notes that are *the same*, and adds their values together. A **slur** connects notes that are *different*, and it doesn't change the value of the note. We just don't have to tongue the notes under a slur.

Tie between notes that are the *same*    **Slur** between notes that are *different*

All you have to do is keep the air going and move your fingers. The notes get kind of connected. Try it!

Little Slurs

Big Slurs

Banana Peel - Octave Slurs up

Watch your step! - Octave Slurs down

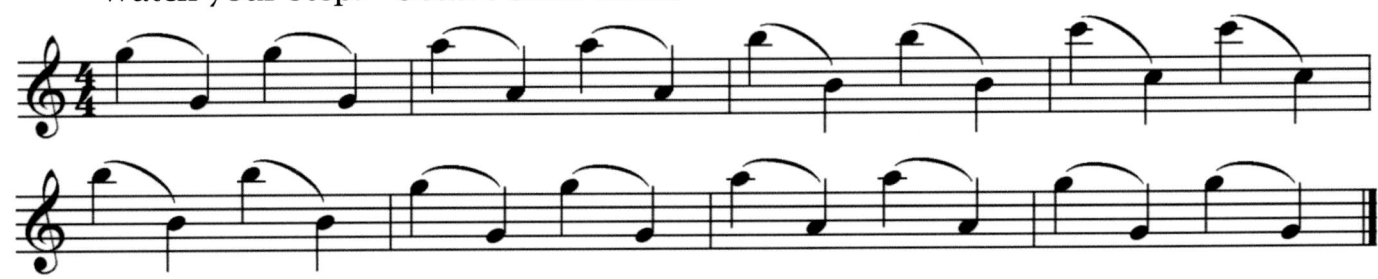

Tunes with Slurs

Chester by William Billings – an early American tune

Theme from Johannes Brahms' *Symphony No. 1*

Triplets

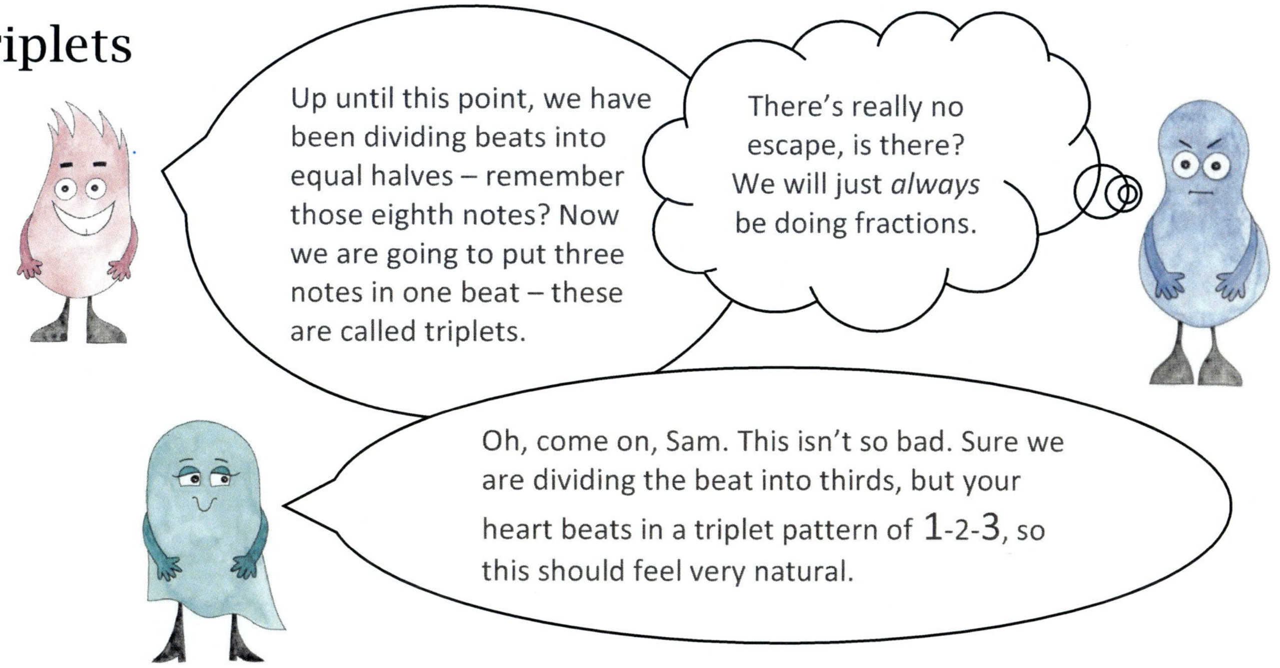

 Up until this point, we have been dividing beats into equal halves – remember those eighth notes? Now we are going to put three notes in one beat – these are called triplets.

 There's really no escape, is there? We will just *always* be doing fractions.

 Oh, come on, Sam. This isn't so bad. Sure we are dividing the beat into thirds, but your heart beats in a triplet pattern of **1**-2-3, so this should feel very natural.

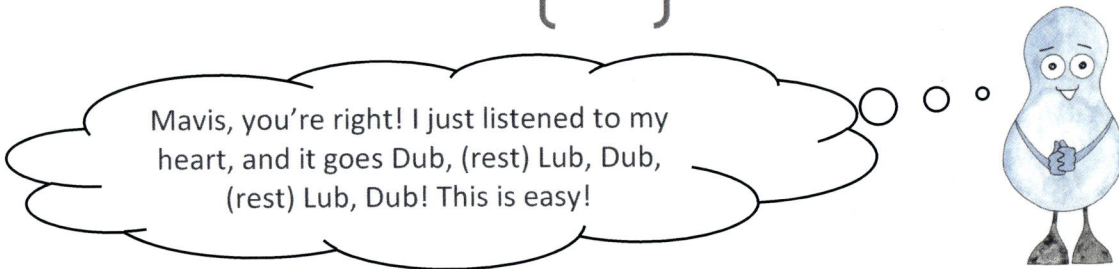

Mavis, you're right! I just listened to my heart, and it goes Dub, (rest) Lub, Dub, (rest) Lub, Dub! This is easy!

Let's try it with some high notes. These two exercises start on high C. Use LOTS of air!

Seasick

St. Columba

This is great! We are learning so much. Since we are talking about triplets, let's learn about **arpeggios**. An arpeggio is a set of notes that, if they were played together would make up a **chord**. We can't play more than one pitch at the same time, so we practice them one after the other.

One of the most common arpeggios is a major arpeggio. This is made up of pitches 1, 3, 5, 8 from the major scale. Keep reading for some arpeggio patterns in several keys we have already learned.

Arpeggios

The same pattern occurs in 5 different scales below. Watch out for the key!

Compound Meter – 6/8

Now that you know about triplets, this should be easy. We're going to talk about 6/8 time, which is a time signature with an 8 on the bottom, not a 4!

Oh, I think I can figure this out. Let's see – there's a 6 on top, so 6 beats in a measure and an 8 on bottom, so the *eighth* note gets the beat!

Wow, Sam! Thanks for explaining that. I was confused by the 8 on the bottom, but I think you got it. Look at the exercises below. They all have 6 *eighth* notes in each measure.

Here's another way to count in 6/8

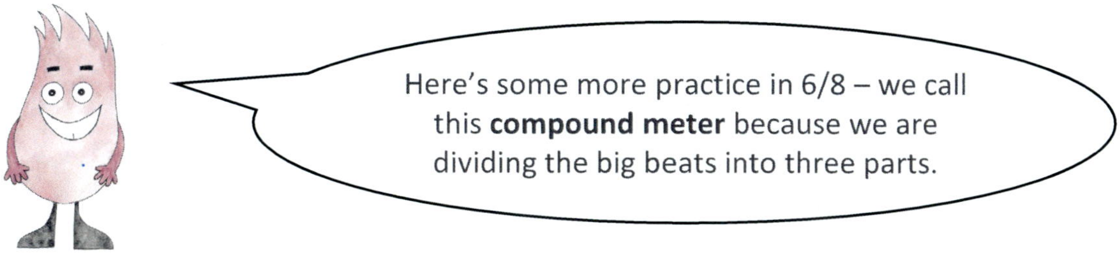

Here's some more practice in 6/8 – we call this **compound meter** because we are dividing the big beats into three parts.

This piece has a **repeat sign**. It looks like this –:‖ Do you see it on the second line? It acts like a trampoline to bounce you back to the beginning, where you start over again. The second time you come to the repeat sign, just keep going.

How Lovely Shines the Morning Star - P. Nicolai

Walking Along the River

On Top of Old Smokey

Cut Time

Look out Sam – here come some more fractions! We are going to talk about **Cut Time**. Cut Time is a shorthand way of writing $\frac{4}{4}$ or **common time** (𝄴) so that we can play really fast. We change the fours to twos and we are off. It looks like this:

𝄵   and means this $\frac{2}{2}$ *Two* beats in a measure

Half note gets the beat

Count the half notes as you go along.

1.  [music staff]
   1 2 1 2   G#!

2. [music staff]
   1 2  +

3.  [music staff]

A French Folk Melody

[music staff]

Recognize this? (No? See p. 32)

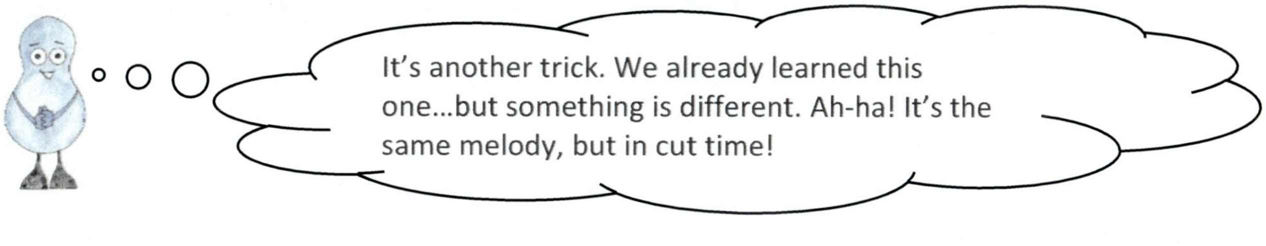

[music staff]

It's another trick. We already learned this one...but something is different. Ah-ha! It's the same melody, but in cut time!

Single Eighth Notes and Rests

Wayfaring Stranger

The Lilting Rowboat

Sixteenth Notes and Beyond!

Up to this point, we have divided the beat into 2s and 3s. Now, we will divide the beat into 4 equal parts! These are called **sixteenth notes** – because there are 16 of them in a 4/4 measure.

We can keep dividing the beat into equal parts as far as we want to – sometimes we see 32nd notes and even 64th notes. Those tend to be *really* fast, so we don't usually go past 64th notes!

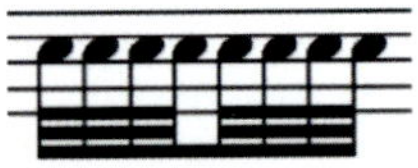

32nd notes   64th notes!

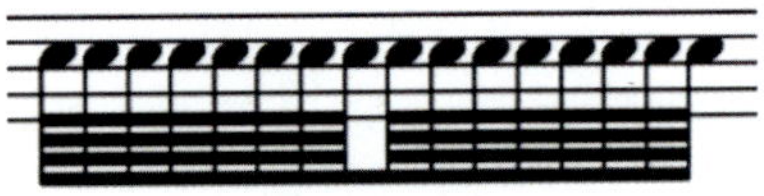

Let's start with something we know – like eighth notes. Each eighth note is equal to **two** sixteenths. Look how they line up.

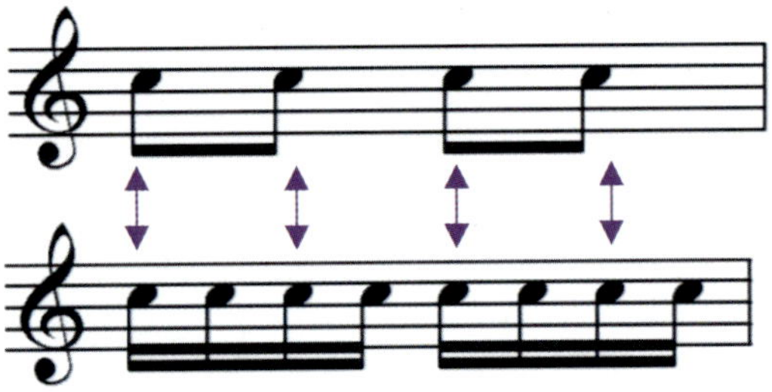

We can do combinations of 8ths and 16ths as well

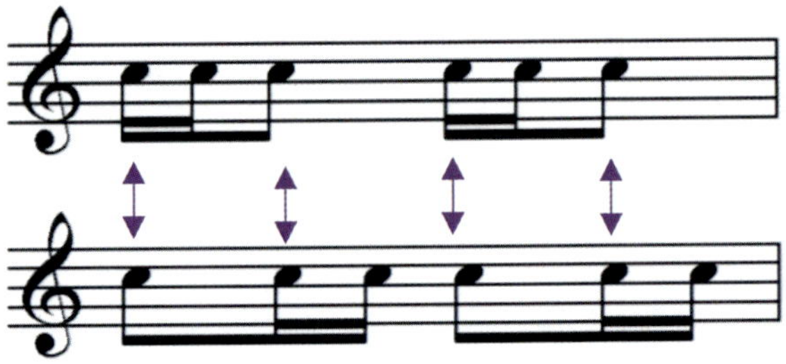

Try it first with just the four sixteenth notes in one beat to get a feel for it.

Mr. Frog Goes to Town

Now try it with these two variations. Be careful, these are not *exactly* the same as the previous one!

Mr. Frog is Full of Hops

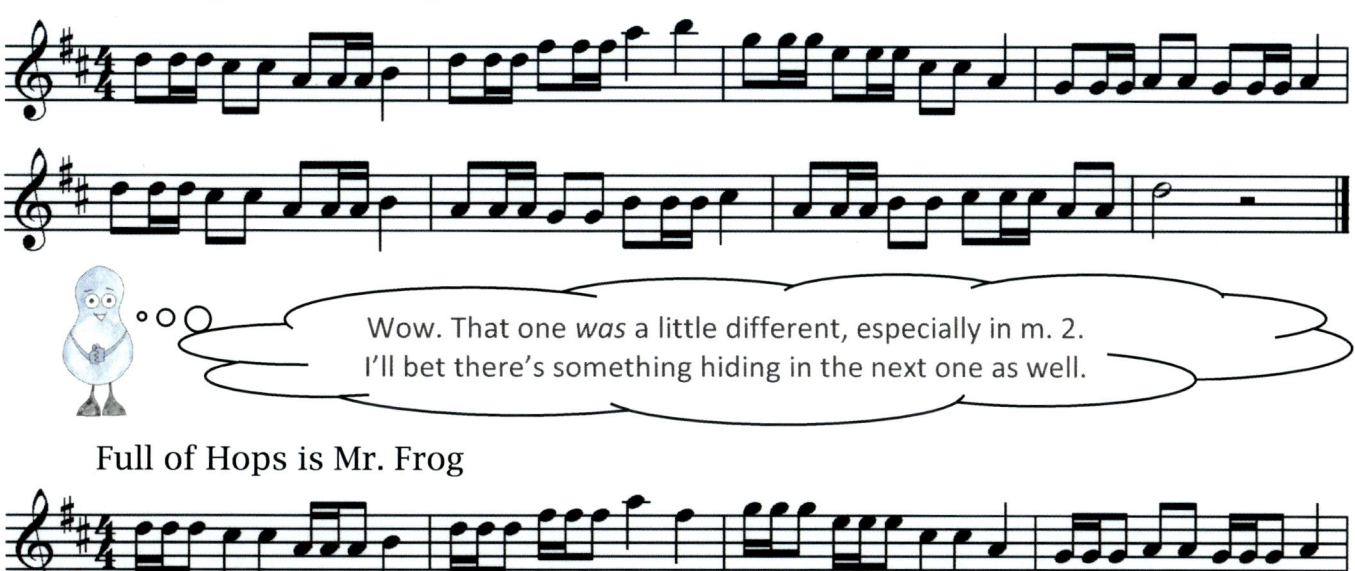

Wow. That one *was* a little different, especially in m. 2. I'll bet there's something hiding in the next one as well.

Full of Hops is Mr. Frog

Counting Challenge: Here's a G major scale that includes all the different types of sixteenth/eighth combinations. Watch out!

How about a duet? This one is called, *Tag, You're It.*

Syncopation and Dotted Eighths

Have you ever learned about ratios in math at school? Well, we have a fancy word for anything with a 1:2:1 ratio: **syncopation.**

Can you remind me what a ratio is? I feel like it's something I've heard of, but I can't remember.

I've got this. A ratio is "the relation between two similar magnitudes with respect to the number of times the second contains the first."

You spend way too much time on Dictionary.com

In musical terms, this means that the second of the three notes is twice as long as the first or the third. For example: ♩ 𝅗𝅥 ♩. Syncopation also throws the strong beats off, causing the weaker beats to be accented. This pattern can go on and on like this rhythm: ♪ ♩ ♩ ♩ ♪ Try it below.

High D!

Here's the same tune written with 8ths and quarters.

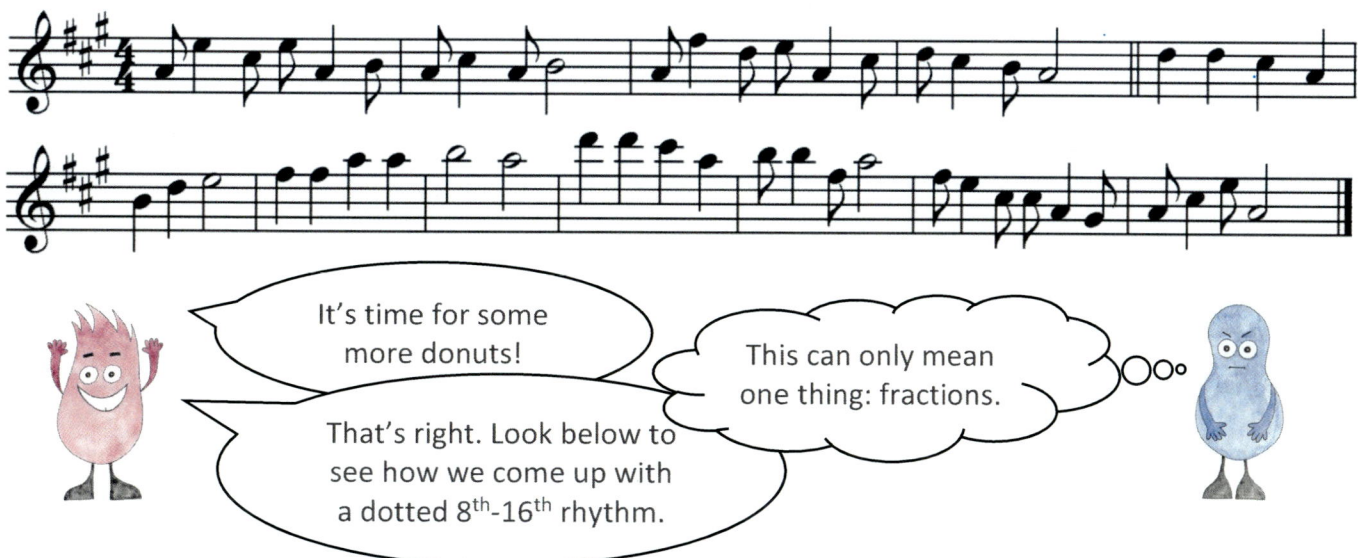

Here it is in donuts, just for you, Sam!
Remember that a dot adds *half* of the value of that note back to itself.

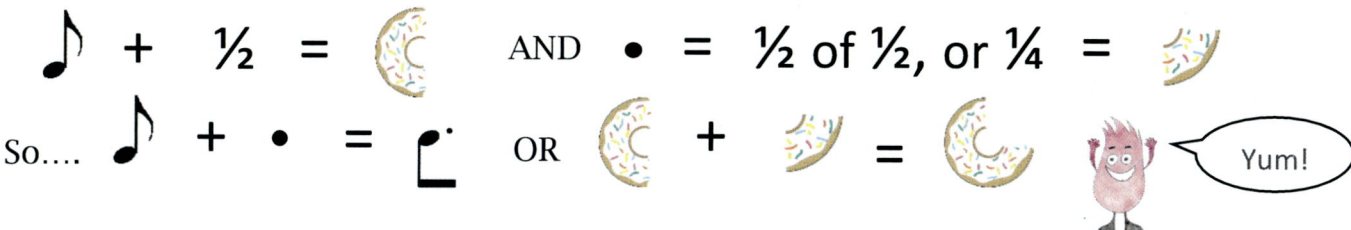

First with ties

Now with the dots

Expanding our Technique Through Time, Key, and Range

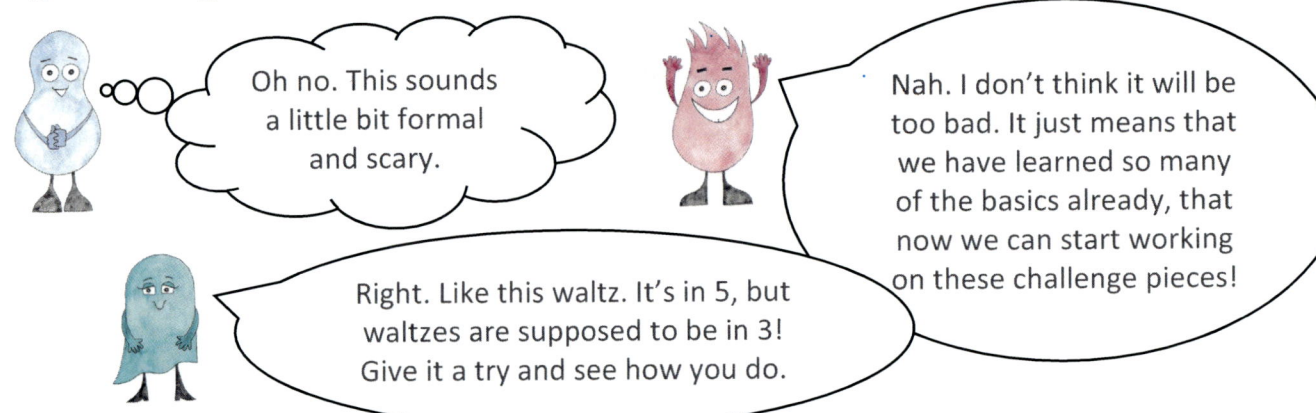

Waltz from the second movement of Tchaikovsky's *Symphony No. 6*

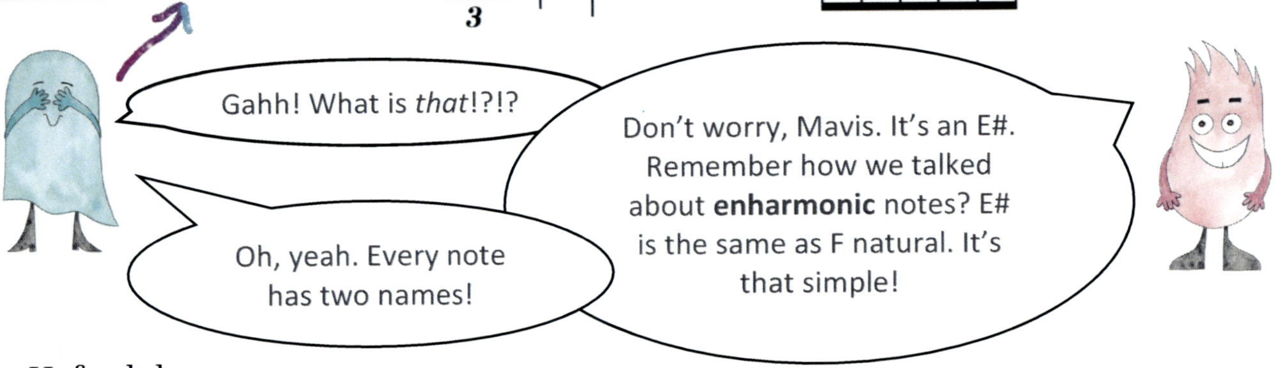

Hyfrydol

These next two pieces are originally written as songs, so think of singing while you play them. They are both trying to paint a picture with their melodies. Can you hear the trout swimming along? Or can you imagine a beautiful morning in May?

The Trout by Franz Schubert

The Lovely Month of May by Robert Schumann

Flutists' Favorites

Flutists have some pieces that they *all* love to play. We have collected a few of them for you here. Have fun learning and playing these!

Badinerie from J.S. Bach's *Orchestral Suite No. 2*

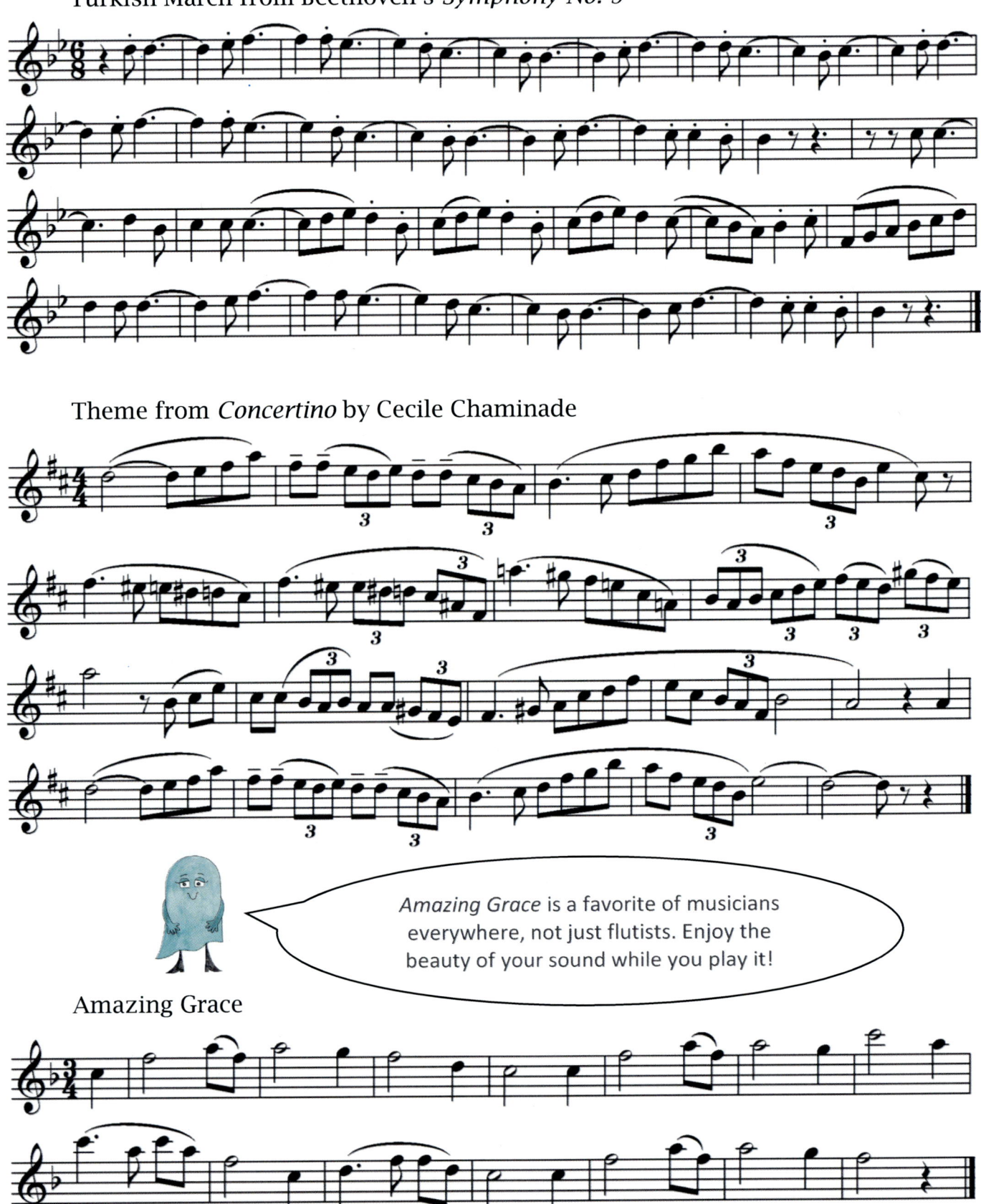

Piccolo solo from *Stars and Stripes Forever* by John Philip Sousa

Overture selections from *Suite in a minor* by George Philipp Telemann

Here are the trills in the order in which they appear in the Telemann. Wiggle the finger where the arrow is pointing.

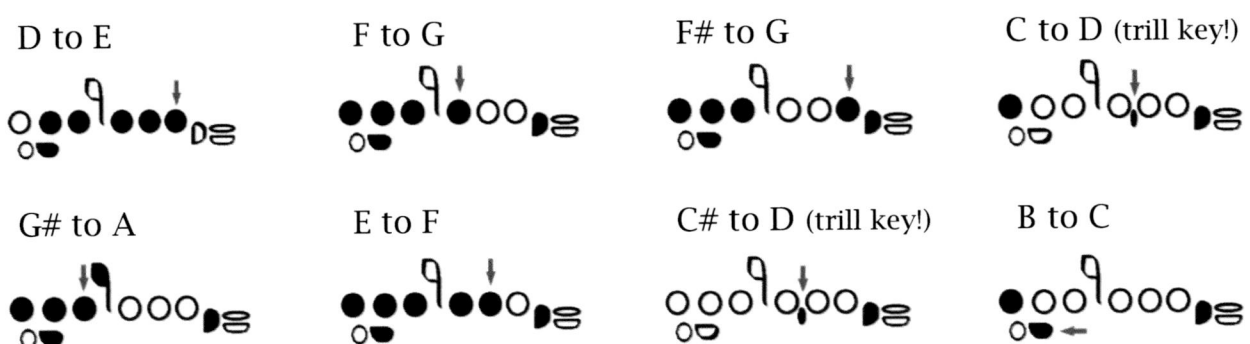

Appendix
(or Extra Stuff at the Back of the Book Used for Reference)

Back here, you'll find several pages of what we hope is helpful information – like a scale sheet or a fingering chart. There's even a glossary of musical terms we used throughout the book, so if you forget what something means, you can look it up. My favorite page, however, is the Circle of Fifths. I just love to look at how the keys are organized.

Vocabulary

arpeggio - a pattern of notes made up of pitches that are usually a third apart. In a scale, we often use pitches 1, 3, 5, and 8. If a piano played all of the notes of an arpeggio at the same time, it would be called a chord.

body (of the flute) - the middle of the three parts of the flute. This piece has most of the keys.

chord - a set of three or more pitches played at the same time - this is not possible on the flute! (why is it in the appendix, you ask? See **arpeggio**.)

circle of fifths - a chart of all 24 major and minor keys and their key signatures, organized in a circle with each key the interval of a fifth from its neighbor (see Appendix).

common time - another way of saying 4/4 time. It is represented by this symbol: **C**

compound meter - any meter or time signature where the large beats are divided into three parts (6/8, 9/8, 12/8, etc). (see **simple meter** too)

crescendo - a musical symbol that means to get louder. ⎯⎯⎯⎯ or *cresc.*

cut time - a time signature that is equal to 2/2, and is represented by this symbol: **¢**

decrescendo - a musical symbol that means to get softer. ⎯⎯⎯⎯ or *decresc.*

dynamics - how loud or soft the music is. We use the symbols *pp, p, mp, mf, f,* and *ff* in the music to indicate volume. We can also use a crescendo or a decrescendo to indicate getting louder or softer.

eighth note/rest - a note or rest that gets half of a beat in quarter note time (like 4/4) or one beat in eighth note time (like 6/8).

embouchure - the way we form our lips to blow the air into the flute.

enharmonics - two notes with different names (look different) but have the same pitch (sound the same) like D# and Eb. They are also the same key on the piano keyboard.

flat - lowers a pitch by a half step and is represented by the ♭ symbol. If you see this in front of the note B, the B becomes B *flat* or B♭.

footjoint - one of the three parts of the flute. This piece connects to the body and only has a few keys pressed by the right hand pinkie.

half note/rest - a note or rest that gets two beats in quarter note time (like 4/4).

headjoint - one of three parts of the flute. This piece is the part we blow into.

key - a set of pitches that form a tonal group. For example, the key of F Major has one flat and centers around F as tonic.

key signature - the place at the beginning of a staff where the key is represented in varying numbers of sharps and flats, based on what the key is.

ledger lines - tiny lines above or below the staff that extend the range of the staff. *(Flutists spend a lot of time reading ledger lines above the staff!)*

lip plate - The part of the headjoint that rests on our chin.

major - a specific collection of notes that form a key area. These notes are organized with the following whole (W) and half (H) steps between them: WWHWWWH (C to D is a whole step, E to F is a half, etc.)

measure - one unit of duration. It includes the number of beats specified by the time signature.

minor - a specific collection of notes that form a key area. These notes are organized with the following whole (W) and half (H) steps between them: WHWWHWW (C to D is a whole step, E to F is a half step, etc.)

musical alphabet - A set of 12 alphabetical letters from A to G representing all of the pitches in music.

natural - cancels out a sharp or flat and is notated with this symbol: ♮

off beat - the unstressed part of a beat. In quarter note time, it's the second eighth note of any beat, or the "and" of 1-and-2-and-3-and-4-and.

pulse - a consistent beat that helps define the tempo and meter of a piece. The pulse can be fast quarter notes in 4/4 time, slow eighth notes in 6/8 time, or even slow eighth notes in 4/4 time.

quarter note/rest - a note or rest that gets one beat in quarter note time (like 4/4).

relative major and minor - scales and key areas that share the same key signature but start on different pitches. For example: d minor is the relative minor of F major. For a whole list of these relatives, see the **circle of fifths** chart.

repeat sign – a musical symbol which tells the performer to go back to another repeat sign and continue playing (or to go to the beginning of the piece if no previous repeat sign exists). It is represented by this symbol: :|

scale – a collection of pitches that outline a key. Some kinds of keys are major, minor, pentatonic, wholetone, chromatic, or modal.

sharp – raises a pitch by a half step and is represented by the # symbol. If you see this in front of the note F, the F becomes F *sharp* or F#.

simple meter – a meter or time signature where the beats are most commonly divided into two (4/4, 3/4, 2/4, etc). (see **compound meter**)

sixteenth note/rest – a note or rest that gets ¼ of the beat in quarter note time. There are 16 of them in a 4/4 measure and that's where they get their name.

slur – a musical symbol (⌒) which extends over two or more notes, causing them to be played in one breath with no articulation other than on the first note. A slur looks like a tie, but a slur is between two or more notes of *different* pitch.

tie – a musical symbol (⌒), which joins the values of multiple notes of the same pitch together. For example, if you have a half note tied to a quarter note, the value of that note is now 3 (2+1=3).

time signature – Determines the meter of a piece and how many beats are in a measure. Some common examples are 4/4, 3/4, 2/4, 6/8.

tonic – the home note of a key – in G major the tonic is G. Likewise, in Eb major the tonic is Eb.

treble clef – also known as G Clef, this helps us determine which lines and spaces are named which letters. The curve of the G clef goes around the G line.

whole note/rest – a note or rest that gets four beats in quarter note time (like 4/4).

Here is a table of common musical terms and their English meaning

Accelerando	Getting faster
Allegretto	A little slower than fast
Allegro	Fast
Andante	Walking tempo
Cantabile	Song-like
Largo	Slowly
Meno	Less
Moderato	Moderate
Piu	More
Poco	A little
Scherzo	Joke-like
Ritardando	Slowing down
Rallentando	Broadening

Order of Sharps and Flats

Curious about key signatures? There's a secret code to figuring them out!

The next couple of pages are resources that center on key signatures and all the places that they pop up. You can find key signatures in the **Circle of Fifths**, in **Scales**, and of course, in all of the music that you play. It's important to understand how they are structured and to be able to figure out which flats and sharps are in which key signatures. Here's a helpful hint:

Flats and Sharps are always given in the *same* order - no matter what. Here's the secret code:

For the order of flats, read left to right; for the order of sharps, read right to left. Lots of people use a sentence to remember the sharps and flats. Try this one or come up with one of your own!

Beautiful **E**lephants **A**re **D**ancing **G**racefully while **C**arrying **F**lowers

So, if we have one flat, it's ALWAYS B♭, and if we have only one sharp, it's ALWAYS F#. Count the number of flats and look at the code above. If there are three, they will be B♭, E♭, and A♭.

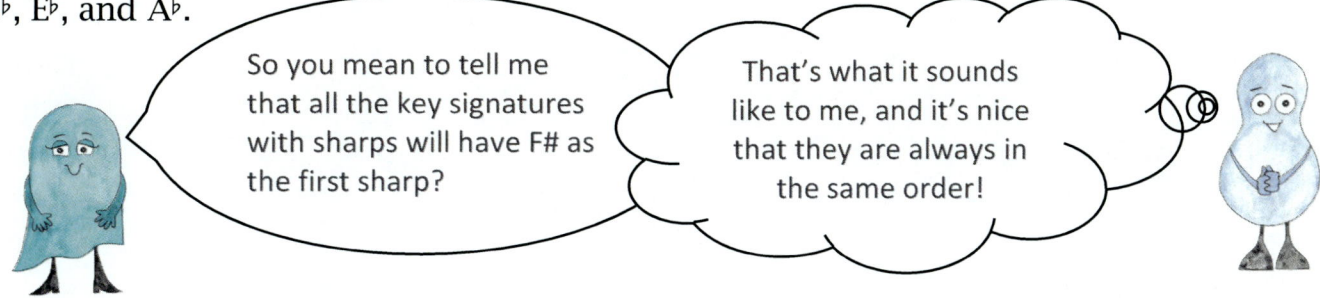

So you mean to tell me that all the key signatures with sharps will have F# as the first sharp?

That's what it sounds like to me, and it's nice that they are always in the same order!

Circle of Fifths

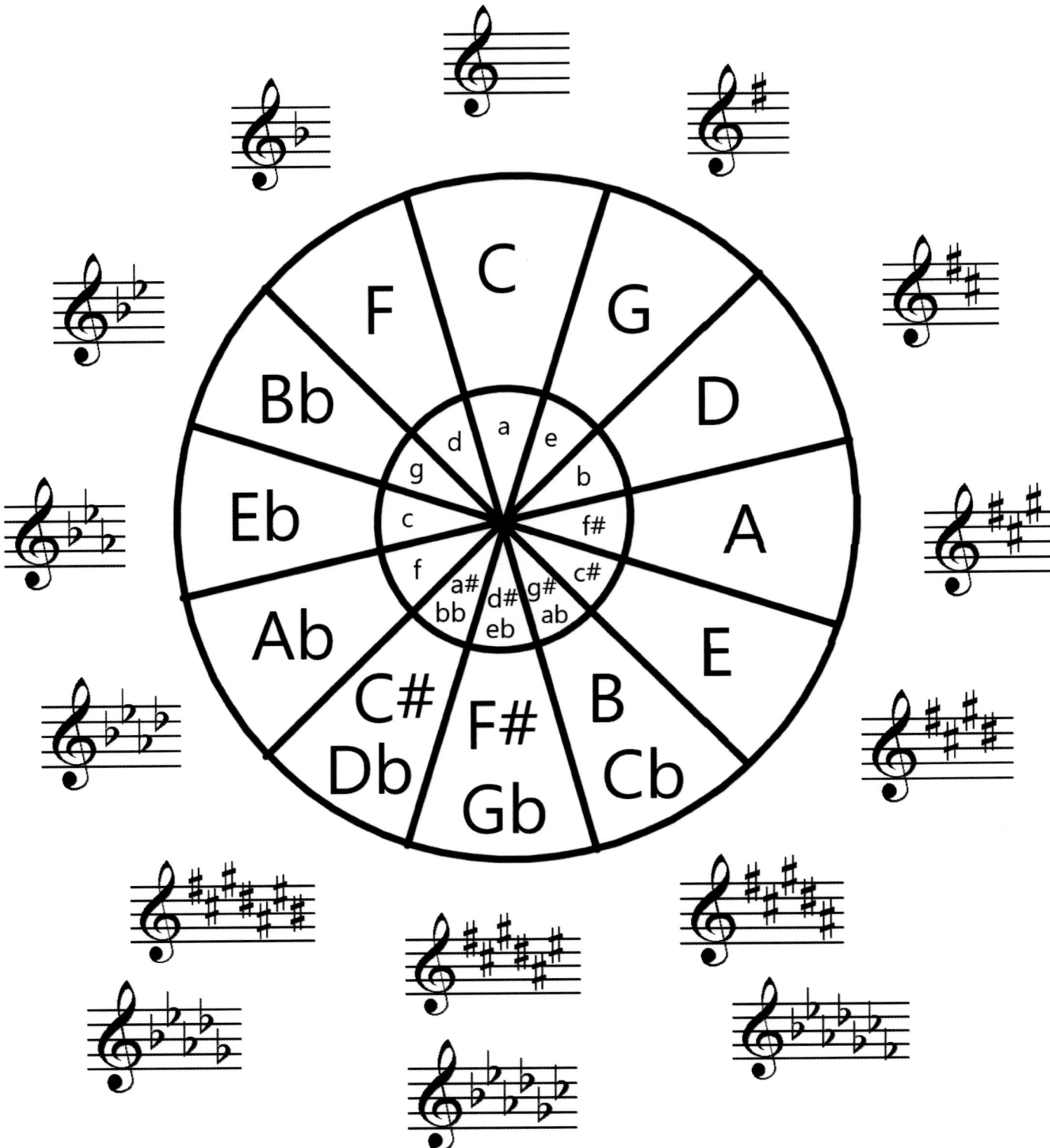

Understanding the Circle of Fifths

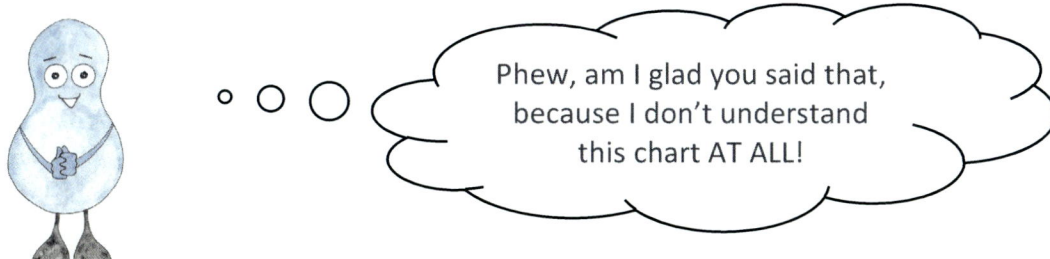

This chart shows us all 12 different key signatures. It is organized to kind of look like a clock. See how there are 12 spaces? We have C Major at the top – it has no sharps or flats. As we go around the circle to the right (clockwise), we have the sharp keys starting with G Major with one, then D with two, and so on, until we get to *seven* sharps (C#).

If we start at C and go to the left (counter-clockwise), we have the flat keys starting with F Major with one, then B♭ with two, and so on, until we get to *seven* flats (C♭).

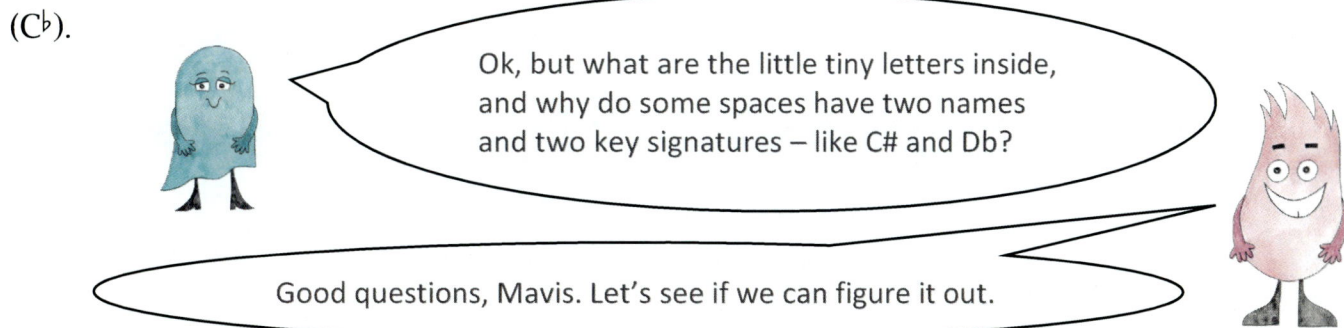

The capital letters are all major keys, so the lowercase letters are all minor keys. Each major key has a **relative minor** key with the same key signature. So A minor has no sharps or flats, and it starts on A.

The three key signatures at the bottom are called **enharmonics.** If you look back at the keyboard picture on p. 22, you'll see that each black key has two names. Here they are! C# and D♭ are the same note, we just sometimes spell them differently. They have so many sharps and flats that we have two different ways to write them. If you closed your eyes, though, they would sound exactly the same!

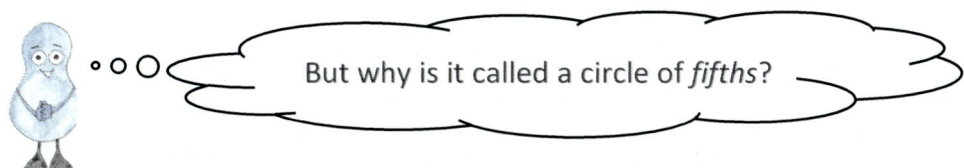

It's called a Circle of Fifths because when you count from C to G you get a fifth. Try it. Starting on C as 1, count up to G (C-1, D-2, E-3, F-4, G-5). And if you count from D to A, you will also get 5. If you keep going, the distance between the key signatures will always be a fifth, all the way back to C. Pretty cool, huh?

Major Scales

Scales are one of the things we use to help our fingers get faster and to teach us about key signatures. There are 12 major scales. It's ok if you can't play the really high or low notes just yet. You'll get there!

C Major

G Major

F Major

D Major

Bb Major

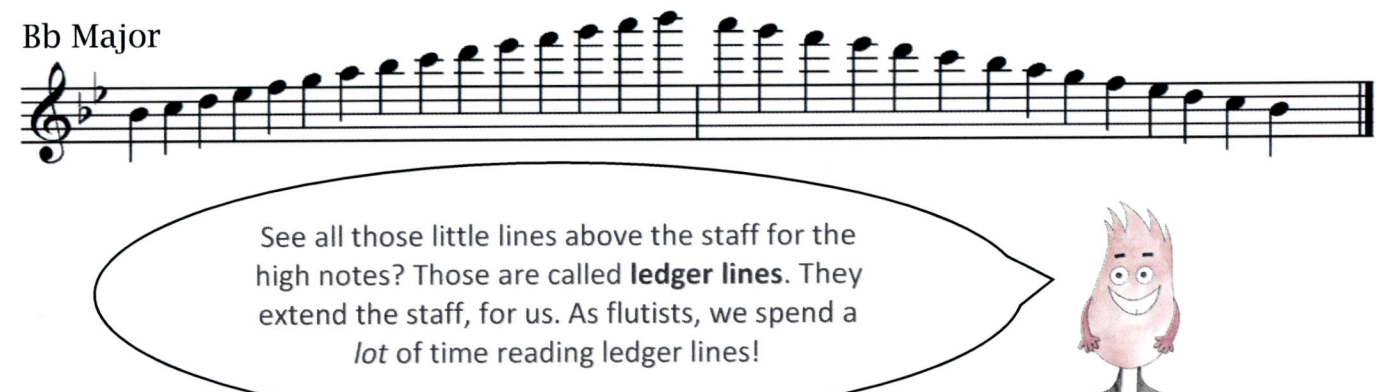

See all those little lines above the staff for the high notes? Those are called **ledger lines**. They extend the staff, for us. As flutists, we spend a *lot* of time reading ledger lines!

A Major

Eb Major

E Major

Ab Major

B Major

Db Major

Gb Major

Fingering Chart

Fingering Chart continued

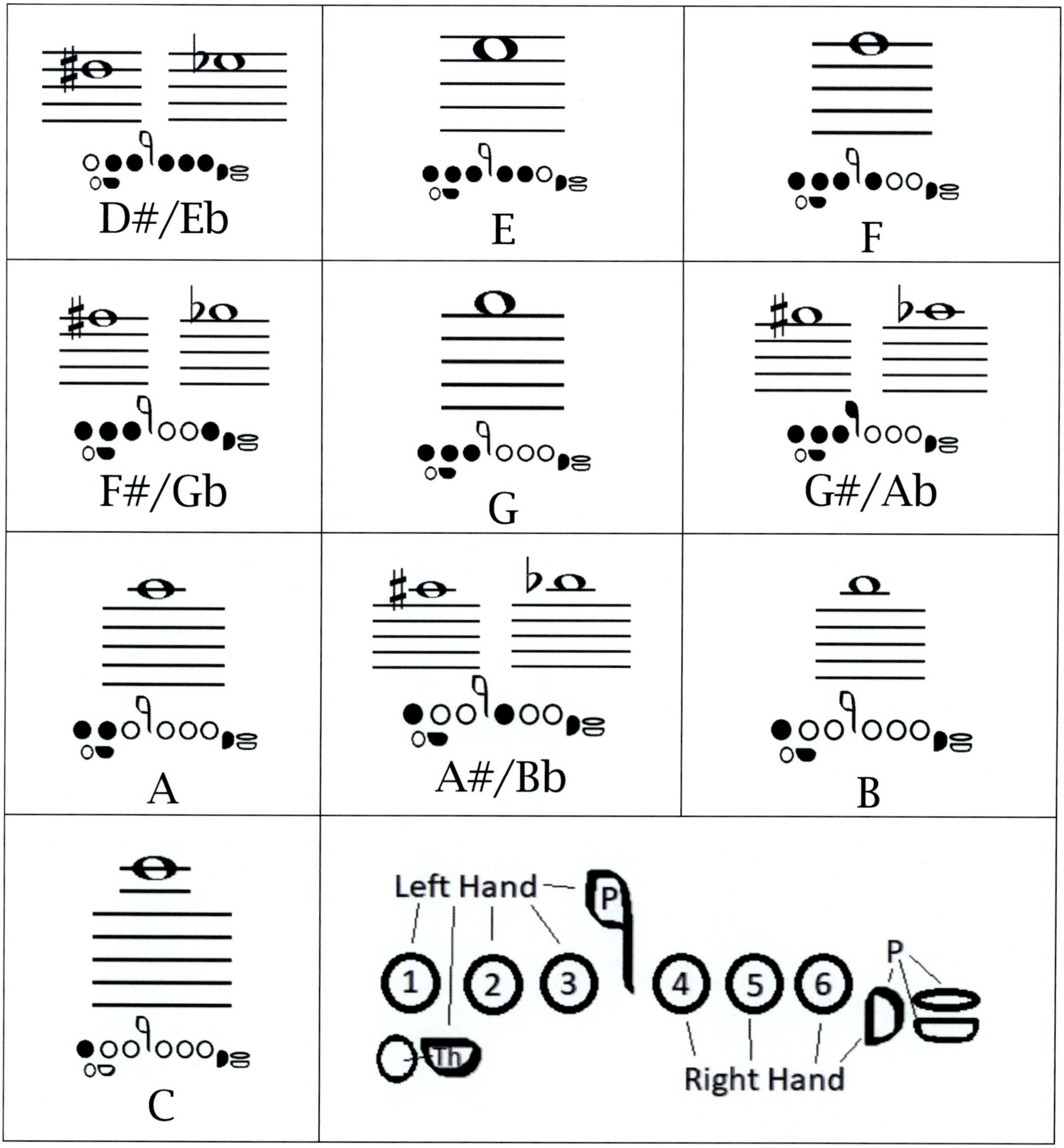

D#/Eb	E	F
F#/Gb	G	G#/Ab
A	A#/Bb	B
C	Left Hand / Right Hand diagram	

*Make sure to notice the one key we skip with our **left hand**. There is a key we don't press down between finger 1 and finger 2. We left it off the fingering diagram, so you didn't get confused.

Flash Cards – Cut out these cards and use them to practice your note reading.

D	C#/Db	C
F	E	D#/Eb
G#/Ab	G	F#/Gb
B	A#/Bb	A

D	C#/Db	C
F	E	D#/Eb
G#/Ab	G	F#/Gb
B	A#/Bb	A

Ciao!

Made in the USA
Middletown, DE
09 February 2020